W9-CNG-057

THERE ARE BIRDS

JOHN TAGGART

THERE
ARE
BIRDS

FLOOD EDITIONS

CHICAGO

Published by Flood Editions

www.floodeditions.com

ISBN 978-0-9787467-7-3

Cover photograph: Ralph Eugene Meatyard,
Untitled, ca. 1968–72. Copyright © The Estate
of Ralph Eugene Meatyard, courtesy
Fraenkel Gallery, San Francisco

Designed and set by Quemadura
Printed on acid-free, recycled paper
in the United States of America

This book was made possible
in part through a grant from
the Illinois Arts Council

THERE ARE BIRDS

REFRAINS FOR ROBERT QUINE

Love comes in spurts. —RICHARD HELL & THE VOIDOIDS

1

And goes is gone
cause for mourning head
in hands in tears gonna be a long long wait for the resurrection
of the dead.

There are birds there is birdsong
unmourning and unmournful at sunrise in the white light
there is a garden with high walls around it
jardin de plaisir
garden of mint and lavender of hyssop in hedges glassy beads of
    water on velvet leaves
purple-flaked lupin spikes above velvet pulmonaria
there is a gardener la belle jardinière bare-breasted and bare-footed
bouquets
of all flowers in her arms and woven in her hair.

2

And it hurts not good but
bad
to see a man head in hands in tears it breaks you up
to see a man come down in tears.

There are birds there is birdsong
having come through hunger and danger
there is free song
a free weaving of many songs
song against song and other songs clustered/spun out in a
    blending of wavy pitches
tant
doucement the phrase means what the songs mean
freshness
that meaning so sweetly and freely as a gardener weaves flowers in
    her hair.

3

Can we stay in the weave of
that meaning can we/should we attempt to stay to linger
in a pleasure garden everlasting dream of
love tomorrow its unseen/secret structure when our time
    remains a
bad time and what
time wasn't bad wasn't and isn't a time of hunger and danger of
    young men and older men
in tears our time a time
of terror and counterterror can
we/should
we our
time remaining a really bad time a really down and dirty time
of terror what
walls do not fall and who says they have no fear.

4

And boo-hoo-hoo
like dolls
hurts breaks you up like dolls get broken the visible human
the visibly spastic plastic.

There are birds there is birdsong
unmourning and unmournful having come through
there is a garden with swept gravel paths
dream designed/bel et bon designed connecting and
    interconnecting
non brisé
where men and women are in contemplation in conversation in
one another's eyes
there is a gardener holding her bouquets and holding her skirts
    like the light like
so sweetly woven song like love never for sale.

GREY SCALE/ZUKOFSKY

To become aware of tones

beginner's problem in the mind of the beginner

visualization of white of whiteness
which is impossible

I saw an egret in a scraggly cedar above
Big Spring

Williams said no whiteness is so white as the memory of whiteness

in a cedar or motionless in water/the tall grasses.

Silver maple woods what Jennifer named
the scary woods
scary so dense and so dark

dense with undergrowth

with heaped-up multiflora rose with jewelweed

damselfly

a or the or neither and darker than
dark

black wings at rest on jewelweed blackness without dots or density.

3

Middle grey

sledgehammer

to break up cast-iron machines
bow saw to cut down weedy box elders shot up around the machines
time

in which to make a cleared space to find limestone/middle grey

Pound said wind is part of the process

rain part of the process.

4

Three tones + other tones

glaring surface of snow in flat sunlight it's white it's a white
    world wilful travelers
without colored and coloring glasses
long gone

snow in full shade
white with delicate textures sand dune ripples any Bach fugue

average snow

average white skin the shadow of a smile

leaves of trees their shadows
no snow

dark material dark fur dark grey cat named "Friendly."

5

Three tones + other tones + two tones

Richard Avedon's 1958 photograph of Pound a postcard a
    bookmark
darker closed
eyes wrinkled texture of sagging skin around eyes

and darker closed lips no texture almost no-tone tone

"but shall have his sorrow for
sea-fare"

two tones

first suggestions/thresholds of his sorrow.

6

The great photographs are black and white and middle grey

Weston
at Point Lobos rock solid shadow of eroded
rock

Ansel Adams at Yosemite and
elsewhere morning star aspen leaves

Stieglitz portraits of Georgia O'Keefe not simply not necessarily
   great

not because of subject matter this is the American

earth and personages.

                              7

The great

result of reduction and the composition of reduction

resulting in intensity Williams
said the only human value = intense

intense face of sorrow
on a postcard

although there are other emotions and although there are other

faces.

8

And so I come
to the
to the one/only photograph on my wall

and am I not one of those travelers a wilful one or merely a
    stubborn one
still stubborn still

come

home to Ralph Eugene Meatyard's 1968 photograph

on my wall.

No eyes/closed eyes

behind large dark glasses darker than leaves of trees their shadows
    larger
made larger/darker by wings/rock eyebrows

the mouth is also closed

unsmiling

face
to shadow face
large on a neck of average white skin.

1 0

No face = no image = no memory

eyes + mouth + what's been overlooked/unremembered
beginner's error

+ an ear for instance

image of intense attention

what I remember = "only song matters"

not one song only but one/only photograph
on my wall.

Call it a cadenza/some traveling music

off the scale

and going/getting past the question of who's the fairest of them all

of them all watching over me

after a or the or

neither.

UNVEILING/MARIANNE MOORE

In the words of Hsieh Ho, the first of the six laws is called
animation through spirit consonance. —KUO JO-HSÜ

1

Skinny tree sparsely branched lacking
a felicitous phrase to begin

bark of the tree snake-barked maple Acer tegmentosum

dark crimson branch tips in winter chalky white striped trunk
    then branches
sparsely
ending in narrow in tapering tips pairs of buds
along the tips

understory tree
its story what's under
her story what's crimson what's white

neither the eiresione nor daphnephoria

not any kind of bringing in the tree story rather the reverse
bringing oneself to the tree

myself to her self in stop and start in stop and restart
   animation/reanimation

in winter when you can see your own breath

sound of one's footsteps in the
snow the only sound.

2

Her story

local girl grew
up around here in this valley

though not born here
born near St. Louis center of the wholesale fur trade before
1921

grew up around here in this valley in the
space between north and south mountain two blue mountains
long waveforms/ridgelines of two blue mountains

in this valley between forms/lines.

3

Surroundings answer questions.

4

Her story

grew up in a row house
a house between other houses all in a row

343 North Hanover

two windows
embroidered lace curtains dog and
cat figurines tiny blue and white vases on the sills

above
two windows one window on the left window of her room
what she could see on a clear day she could see north mountain

and if she couldn't see it she could feel it

some of the houses all in a
row are stuck together no space between them

between 343 and 345 a narrow passage leading to a narrow back
   yard

no space and/or narrow

man who lives in the house now says there's an underground
tunnel from the cellar to what
was a stable

says 95% of the town don't know who she was who she

was what she was
between.

5

Combination of noun and adjective
binomial

substantive and modifier of the substantive

Acer = maple + tegmentosum
= covered
two Latin words noun and adjective for one thing the tree
and its covering leaves

noun for genus for family adjective for species one particular
    member
of the family

Carl Linnaeus his system for naming things
whose father renamed himself after a tree himself
Linnaeus after the
linden

system for naming and for classifying
bringing things into relation with other things other plants and
animals

multiplying contact

no system no
understanding of the world sum total set of names and things the
    world the
total set "the larger beauty"

a system an effort to tell the truth.

6

Another/other effort
the no system apparently no system of the vernacular the
    common
names

snake-barked

16

obeying unapparent rules the rules of
ordinary/extraordinary discourse
when it is extraordinary

saying one thing is another
overstatement of identity not A = A the nonstatement/pseudo-
    statement of
"true identity" but A = B saying one thing is another
truer statement of identity when it is truer

one of the rules
apparently saying one and another = the same

which gets your attention which
is another rule

as a snake gets your attention

"my hasty steps were suddenly stopped"

William Bartram the first native-born American
to devote his entire life to the study of nature
who traveled through North and South Carolina Georgia East and
    West Florida the
Cherokee country the
extensive country of the Muscogulges or Creek Confederacy and
    the country
of the Chactaws who was suddenly stopped by a rattlesnake

his entire life 1739–1823 in the travels of that life
devoted to the study of nature

stopped
compelled to pay attention

to get you to stop to pay attention vivid bark
of a tree made more so

made truer/more vivid/unveiled A having been veiled however
momentarily by B
which is another rule the veiling to be unveiled rule

the veiling taking place in the fusion

see the A see the B see the A-B the fusion see the A through the B
see the A better more vividly
see A
finally/at last
unveiled

unapparent rules and motivations of ordinary discourse

A = the bark of a tree B = the skin of a
snake

his painting of a rattlesnake ripple and shimmer black brown and
    white shimmering
in a pattern of small leaves in a coiled leafy pattern
William Bartram paid attention

to know one thing
white vertical strips grey-green patches

another thing/other things must be
known paid attention to known and brought together hyphenated
    fused
A-B which is
another rule the intense fusion however momentary so that the
first is the last thing that gets your attention.

7

Another/other effort the common names

identification
precedes understanding of
the world the sum total set of names and things

identification
of one thing through another thing

and attention precedes the painting of identification

color and pattern preceding Crotalus horridus color and pattern and
the not in Latin rattle.

8

"Curious men"

18th century common
name for botanists naturalists horticulturists all the attentive
students of nature.

9

The truth is naked

the truer truth is the A after B truth the figurative/the body
after finally/at last without
a stitch.

1 0

A new name a true name unpublished not
in the books

nomen nudum a naked name.

11

My story

bringing oneself to the tree
oneself/myself to her and a mystery

oneself/myself a detective in a mystery story

what a detective does
identifies the body identifies who done it to the body

what a detective does
asks questions was she the pale pale blonde with anemia of some
    non-fatal but
incurable type was she in the know about snakes.

12

Her story in her own words

"When I was sixteen—in fact thirteen—
I felt as old as any time since and what I wish
I could have been when sixteen I am trying to be now . . .

. . . took a day
at a time . . . because I had to . . .

. . . regarded myself as a wallflower . . . did not like my face . . . many
of my 'best clothes' . . .

introvert."

13

Introvert = inward turned inward in
no space/a narrow space

what can be done in a narrow space you can
read.

14

A classics illustrated comic book the classically animated fables of
La Fontaine
will fit in a narrow/thin space between the thin
pages of a bible or of a hymnal between the brotherhood
and service hymn tunes.

15

A comic book

"juxtaposed images in deliberative sequence"

images = clear A after B pictures

in = the space between white space and spaces in the
head

sequence = one after
another set of things that belong together that are put together
that are made to hold together

local girl bark of a tree skin of a snake

no causality or a different causality

repetition of a phrase a unit/part of a melody at a higher or lower
    pitch
a phrase-mark a line linking notes that belong together
dependence of a subordinate verb according to rules of tense for
    the principal verb

the principal verb is think

deliberative sequence a line of thought
which is not a straight line which is branching/serpentine
linea
serpentinata

which stops and starts/restarts which has a life
a form of its own cut up or broken
nonetheless a life form rhythm
of its own.

16

Who studied all the painters around/before him the northern and
   the southern the
three landscape schools

who traveled among all the rivers and all the mountains

then stayed put cleansing himself

who painted the handscroll "10,000 Crazy Dots"

Tao-chi most
apparently unsystematic of all the systematic painters of China

Tao-chi said the line/i-hua
the line is the basis of all things and the root of myriad
   phenomena

broken or dotted the basis the root.

17

"Has form"

Brit cop-talk for repeat offender suspect
with a criminal record suspected of offending/committing a
   crime the
same or similar again.

18

Advertisement at the back/last page of
a comic book
send for x-ray vision glasses

see the A better a more vivid/unveiled body in the body of the
    world beauty in
the larger beauty

at last

Tao-chi said vision should/must be penetrating.

19

Reading and writing require focusing the mental attention upon
a text by means of the visual sense. As an individual reads and
writes he gradually learns to close or inhibit the input of his
senses, to inhibit or control the responses of his body, so as to
train energy and thought upon the written words. He resists the
environment outside him by distinguishing and controlling the
one inside him. This constitutes at first a laborious and painful
effort for the individual . . . In making the effort he becomes aware
of the interior self as an entity separable from the environment
and its input, controllable by his own mental action. The recogni-
tion that such controlling action is possible, and perhaps neces-
sary, marks an important stage . . . a stage at which the individual
personality gathers itself to resist disintegration.

20

He = an individual she the
environment = surroundings = forms/lines of two blue mountains.

21

Gradually learns = how
to hum along with the hymn tunes with
the out of tune congregation the church crowd noise

how to hum along
and be thinking gradually learning

how to think for herself/all by herself an individual she self

how to hum along and be thinking about the classics the news that
    stays news
about the news of an animal fable the human
animal news.

22

Gradually learns = laborious and painful like giving birth.

Gradually learns = how
to hum along with the out of tune and hum one's
own tune
at the same time

a little tune in another/romance language
language

"Une jeune fillette" a mélodie populaire a pop tune

like humming along with
"teach me my god and king" and humming "teach me tonight"

thinking not of course of the ABC/XYZ of it but the
A = B of it the veiled to be unveiled
of it a/the fabulous young girl

like humming along with
"in all things thee to see" and humming "I only have eyes for you"
and thinking of you a/the fabulous young girl
and thinking of how an individual she/herself could become
    you a/the fabulous
young girl.

24

Gradually learns = how
to read in church and not only in church how to
read between all the forms/lines of a valley this local environment.

25

And not only in church

when alone in her room whether or not on a black bearskin rug how
   to read
naked/nakedly.

26

Elbows at cradle angles

a young woman on her side reading
on a red blanket
theater/movie sidelighting flat black background

slenderella arms and slenderella fingers highlighted a frame of sorts

cradling/framing one breast foreshortened bulge warm bowl that's
   been tilted

its shadow on the white pages
of a book

a Picabia picture to illustrate this gradual picture of reading

red is an emotional color the space between her edges and the
     book's edges an emotional
space.

2 7

Gradually learns = a day at a time.

2 8

Humming

a continuous low sound a singing with closed lips

a sound coming from the interior
of the body as the sound of a violin comes from the interior/the
cavity

andantino cantabile.

A detective asks questions

where's the tree from when it's at home did the first native-born
nature boy find it

from another valley Amur
river valley in northeast China on the border with
Siberia

Amur in Siberia Heilung Kiang in China black dragon river in
  China

not found by William Bartram nor by E. H. "China" Wilson most
  intrepid nature
boy but intrepid in western China
climbed Mt. Omei one of the five sacred mountains where he
saw Acer davidii
on his way to the top "the golden summit"

Acer davidii another snake-barked maple

named after Père Armand David who found it also
found the dove tree found
Davidia involucrata

hanging white bracts hanging down/all over the dove tree also
  called by another

common name the handkerchief tree
which got the most intrepid nature boy started on his intrepid
way in the flowery kingdom mother of gardens China

sent by the Royal Exotic Nursery sent from England 1899
to collect seeds of the dove tree also
handkerchief tree

a white tree got him sent/started

white
the motive.

30

If the tree's home is China
then how to come to the tree when my home is in this valley
    between
two blue mountains

plant the
tree in this/my own valley

not the single/same tree found in 1850 by a Russian
nature boy in the Amur/black dragon river valley descendant of
    that same tree

brought into cultivation in 1895

into cultivation something planted/cared for sometimes
called by another name cultivar nickname
added to the Latin name

Acer tegmentosum "White Tigress"

William Bartram said "planting promises a more lasting pleasure."

3 1

But isn't this wrong
to plant a tree from one valley in another
people in one valley know that people in other valleys if
there are other valleys are
suspicious around here "you can't be too careful"

but isn't this wrong

to plant a tree from one valley in another but Asa Gray "the father
of American botany" said no

the one the other were once/long ago the very same/connected
  valley

otherwise how explain why the trees of China northeast America
  are the same trees
and growing nowhere else

Asa Gray said a continuous temperate floristic unit ranged
from Asia to North America only broken by
later/long ago geologic events which
means no separate creation in two valleys what's
found now in two valleys what's descended from one from groves
    of the one tree

later differences = change over time
1859 Asa Gray

but isn't this wrong

to plant a tree from one valley in another

isn't this wrong when a snake-barked maple already grows here
Acer pennsylvanicum native
tree high
up in clumps/clusters along the ridgelines in this valley in this
    state a state of
woods Pennsylvania

first in conservation because it was the first to cut down its
woods and now nearly first of the states in
tonnage of out-of-state garbage
taken in hauled in by
endless thundering trucks to fill its landfills the land filled with
    garbage

Pennsylvania is a careless state few if
any old growth/first growth forests remaining in the careless state
    of Pennsylvania

the tall standing Tuscarora hemlocks the standing dead

but isn't this wrong to
plant the suspicious the exotic the foreign with
the native

Asa Gray said no and I say what's
native is what grows where it's planted however it was planted and
trees are not garbage.

3 2

Where is Pennsylvania

in the state of mind of/careless love mood of Appalachia.

3 3

There are snakes and snakes around here

eastern or timber rattler
silent even more dangerous because silent/no rattle copperhead
of the Viperidae family the most highly evolved of snakes

come out
at the first thunderstorm on
ledges/outcrops of north and south mountain

"if the snake's head is fatter than the neck, it's most likely
poisonous"

what the president of the Keystone Reptile Club said
at the Second Annual Snake Hunt and Outdoors Weekend around
here

and there are snakes in the cellars of old
houses

oikouros ophis

where the pipes/wires
are where the green glass Ball jars are stored in rows on unpainted
wooden shelving
under-sense of fruit and root smell

the jars the pithoi

the pithoigia is the opening of
jars letting ghosts out and thanking the snake for protecting the
jars

wife of the man at 343 says there are
ghosts in the house she once saw a snake in the cellar.

3 4

There are blondes and blondes
no joke
who have their uses not as jokes as aiding in contrast as aiding and
    abetting
clarity

red/auburn-haired she wasn't a blonde
belonged to the league of
red-headed women

who have profound needs

Emily D. a red-headed woman said she had a freckled bosom
freckles a
profound need

to veil freckles to be veiled to be unveiled vividly white
crimson and white Beatrice colors.

3 5

What is it about bosoms wondered Bill Slider the detective
inspector

Maigret another detective on a case in Holland wondered what did a
young woman have to entitle her to play a star
part in a murder mystery drama

two
"two fine round buxom breasts . . . palpitating with life"

two breasts = bosom = part of the body

part of/for the whole
body

which is metonymy identification
of the whole body by a part of the body metonymy another
way of saying one
thing is another thing the whole body thing

the Linnaean system for naming things/identification
not limited to trees

mammal = animal of the class Mammalia having
    mammae/breasts

Linnaean/Latin name for the human among other
things/animals in the class the family.

3 6

Metonymy

a tone a little tune
coming from the interior of the body identifying
what's truly mine/me

"mammals vary in their use of vocalization but, like birds, they
regularly have highly developed interior sound organs . . .

. . . voice becomes more operative
as we move up the evolutionary scale and . . . bodily structure
    somehow becomes more
resonant"

more operative and/or more operatic

the evolution of opera singing is from speech to cry

"the great lyric displays of female singing are located in the zone
of ultimate unintelligibility, in the upper and

extreme upper register of the voice"

a low tone a little
tune she wouldn't cry on command she wouldn't be commanded.

3 7

"Just the facts, mam"

radio
later black and white TV detective sergeant Friday

mam = short for madam among other things a woman operating
    a bordello

around here that's Bessie's House 20 East Locust Avenue in
    continuous operation
since Civil War days six days a week
11 a.m.–2 a.m.
"a fine old institution" operated by Bessie Jane Jones her
mother by her grandmother before her

until October 1 1972 when
Bessie was found bound gagged and dead from a knife wound

dead = in the house blues

just the mam/mammalian facts of life and of
death.

3 8

"... only the names have been changed to protect the innocent"

the innocent = what can be
hurt/injured

as the roots of trees the branches in planting

if the roots are not kept cool/moist
carefully teased pulled free from the rootball fanned
out the soil firmed around them first by the palm then the heel
    deeply watered

before and after
the firming mulched

if a big hole wasn't dug to begin with
cutting away root competition the insidious ghost roots
of other/older ghost trees

avoiding soil contaminated by mystery/mysterious diseases
the sickness of sick rose sickness
avoiding or waiting a long number of years

if the branches weren't carefully tied in with twine to begin with.

3 9

What can be hurt/injured trees
can be

by harsh winds by ice storms one after the other dead summers of
    heat and drought
cankers and rust
enwrapped/clinging all over poison ivy
the ravenous parasites the grubs the borers the beetles
deer damage leaving shattered branches leaving the bark in shreds
    and
in tatters
lightning leaving gashes which go much deeper

by neglect lack of care/cultivation

trees can be hurt/injured
by words a lack of
words or bad news words uttered in a soap opera-ish voice.

4 0

My story stop and start/restart system of
animation a
rhythm system

rheo = to flow as water

which flows in a temporal dimension which flows in
time

which must be stopped if there's to be attention identification
   understanding

the possibility of understanding the inscape and outscape what's
in what
sticks out/edges in the
landscape what sticks out in the winter landscape

gignoke d'oios rhuthmos anthropous echei

rhuthmos = rhythm

41

a rhythm holds men/me one of the anthropous a temporal
dimension

me the junior detective accidental nature boy having
bad eyes and less than wise

what holds me

a time/story line which must be made to stop before restarting
    before there can be

time out of time for
attention identification for the possibility of understanding
anything some one thing a tree in the total set the world in the
    larger
beauty of the landscape.

4 1

In "Potato Head Blues" Louis Armstrong takes a
stop-time chorus

which is when the blues rhythm stops/lays out a chorus a solo a
    new free life floating
free from inside and free from/between the start and
restart of the rhythm.

Chorus the
main body of a pop tune distinct from the verse.

I wonder what is it about white

white "of a clarity beyond
the facts"

clarity what's clear a tree from the forest of
trees a white/clear tree in the forest and against the forest
background a white/clear tree against the nonclear all the local
    colors

not beyond or beyond as after facts

as after the facts of Rousseau's painting the woman
the forest after the forest the surprising woman hands up framing
    her bosom

there's a snake in her hair and hanging down over her shoulders

roussâtre hair over her shoulders and down to her knees

framing and outlining her white
body

after the forest + a lake or river a mountain a hunter shooting a
    black bear with sharp
claws + at sunset

edges of her white body.

4 4

As after the facts of another/other painting the facts of "La
    connaissance naturelle"

c-shadows
of what sticks out
crescent moon shadows Rapunzel hair cascading over her
    shoulders
a forest mountains the sky

although the face has grown older

what naturally sticks out what naturally continues to stick out in
    the mind.

4 5

Older man's one word of advice to the young "curiosity"

two words to those who find themselves not
so young "keep planting."

4 6

Hair/frames/outlines hold together bring out edges and edges
as shadows bring out the clarity of
the clarity of white.

4 7

White of "mine
by the right of the white election"

mine = me a name I call myself self-given naked name
given to one's self by oneself
given as elected as chosen as self-chosen

a self an entity separable from the environment the forest all the
    local colors

the environment this valley between two blue mountains

the environment house in a row of houses a church a continuous
    operation
what's around here

the right to choose a white/clear naked self.

4 8

John Bartram father of William Bartram
also a nature boy also
traveled through North and South Carolina Georgia where
he found Franklinia alatamaha the
Franklin tree
its small white flowers gold dazzled centers never to be found in
the wild again
made observations on the manners of the Indians on
the Indian nymphs

"they would make as handsome, dutiful, industrious, loving, and
faithful wives as many of our own women if
we could whiten their skin a little."

4 9

White
the motive

of red-headed women with the profound need
to veil their freckled bosoms

bosoms parts of/for their whole bodies and selves/souls

the profound need to choose names/selves

for themselves for their own individual
souls the profound need to choose to become not wives but
      nymphs those
who live with/within
trees

choose to become choose to change over time
a day at a time.

5 0

White
the motive of nature boys however shadowed by rejection by
      failure and flight

their motive the desire motive

desire to penetrate the no less profound need to penetrate
all that is veiled.

5 1

"… attention animated by desire is the whole foundation …"

5 2

"... an image ... the very existence of which hangs upon an act of
... attention ..."

5 3

"... and it is desire that saves."

5 4

There are penetrations and penetrations

the difficult/the thrust that must go through to white and

"above all ... thought should be
empty, waiting, not seeking anything, but ready to receive in its
     naked truth the
object that
is to penetrate it"

the object it
could be a white body

the remembered voice of a white body uttering your own naked
     name
going through and through you causing you to
tremble.

5 5

Another detective chief inspector Chen Cao head of the special
   case squad
homicide division Shanghai

"In an investigation, one important link is motive."

5 6

Marlowe private investigator a private
eye

"You've got a case . . . maybe far more than I hear . . . Motive,
   opportunity . . ."

5 7

An investigation = following the tracks the lipstick traces
link = white and T. S. Eliot.

5 8

A case = relation

a case and cases the nominative
the subject the tree the she of her story + the he of my story the

accusative motion coming
to the tree to her the genitive of aim and of
departure

one of the rules there should be agreement there should be some
     concord

the tree the she
what's the aim what's the to be departed from

to come further/far into the woods further/far into memory

to a body
to an intense face.

5 9

Her story taking the opportunity with propriety to
read in church

between chapter and verse the classic
comic book version of the fable of the mouse metamorphosed
     into a maid

a girl and real about fifteen and fabulous

white body skirt of leaves mountain behind her
flowering shape beside her a tree shape crimson red
buds

opportunity to get the picture
fabulous girl.

60

A contrary picture to illustrate the picture a
"mechanical" drawing

"Portrait d'une jeune fille américaine dans l'état de nudité" a
    spark plug marked
FOR-EVER.

61

Point vs. picture

point of the fable the moral the
girl was really a mouse after all and attracted to fur/a rat
fur loves fur/a rat

the moral what's in the
bubble "we are what we were at birth."

6 2

Opportunity with
propriety with some a little

to read the fable in church in her own way front to back and back
to front to A after B humming along and thinking about A
about A after B flipping the pages but with
propriety

and not only in church

front to back and back to front until the moving
pictures become
one vivid/unveiled A after B picture.

6 3

There's a problem an A = A problem with
the fable it's not true
it's a nonstatement it's a pseudo-statement of not enough/not
    true enough identity
to say A mouse in the end
= A mouse

there's a problem with the fable
with the magician who did it in the fable it the magic of
    metamorphosis

mouse
didn't the maid didn't do it

the magic saying one thing truly identified as that thing can
    become another/different
truly identified the A thing can
become the B thing when what's really being said is one
thing is really just
that one thing which as any young woman reader around here
will tell you "that's ignorant"

can become can change over time but
not a long time

a magician is fast mouse in
the hat/girl pops out of the hat the maid/a girl who's really a
    messed up blob
of squeaking fur

like that other classic comic book
girl becomes a tree after a not very long chase her river
father the magician and the chaser who isn't
her father he said it happened real fast just like that and who gets
    excited
about bark

metamorphosis = change over time a long time like
all of your lifetime

there's a problem with the fable with that fast
old black magic that now you see/now you don't magic a problem
with not seeing after the magic

without clarity after

metamorphosis = change over a long time = veiling for the
truer magic the white/clear unveiling

there are problems and problems
freckles don't go away fast.

6 4

There's a problem with that other comic book with
the chaser who's not the truth
who's not naked

who's not the true motive for unveiling which is chosen/self-
    chosen and
chosen again in the self's own time

how do you know you've chosen unless you've chosen again
and again

unless you're persistent

he's no glad day

let him keep his Bernini drapery on let him leave it alone.

6 5

Leonardo used see-
through images exploded views multiple perspectives

now scanning mechanisms powerful microscopes molecular
    surveillance
tools graphics computers generate
"pictures so lifelike ... metaphors may no longer be useful"

that day will never come

mammary gland cells = veined butterfly wings cells of the small
glands around the nipples = accumulations
of berries

wings + berries parts of/for.

6 6

Emily D. said "berries are nice!"

55

Metamorphosis = metaphor over time

metonymy = a little tune in a low tone/song of the cells a part of
metaphor over time.

Graham Stuart Thomas "the world's greatest
gardener" yet another nature boy one of the few men to have a
    rose named
after/with his name

"It is not until one has watched natural growth year by year that
    one begins to understand
the meaning of patience and all the good it brings. If we learn
    this we shall find ourselves
looking with equanimity on the apparent slowness of trees."

Point vs. picture she went for the long run with the picture
the long reanimation of the picture

went by herself for
her self

the picture
white/clear fabulous girl

as any young woman growing up around here will tell you
mountain laurel is the official state flower of the state of
    Pennsylvania
but it's a flower/not a tree don't
you see there's a crimson-branched tree in the
picture.

7 0

There can be pictures under
pictures tones under
tones

there can be one picture there can be one tone

a body an intense face

a convulsive crying like the crying of a child who's been beaten
    been left
in a dark room

what's under all the pictures and all the tones what gives depth
    and what gives
definition.

Didn't go for *Gems from the Poets*
1894 "profusely illustrated"

introduced by Dr. Cuppy "there is something of poetry born
in each of us . . .
for the world is full of roses, and the roses full of
dew, and the dew is full of heavenly love that drips for me and you"

didn't go in for all that drippy fulfilment

after all the girl in the picture
the walking in beauty picture wasn't walking was holding an
empty basket empty
not full

she had walked from Holly to Boiling Springs nine miles is no
    mean stroll

Mount Holly Springs to Boiling Springs wooded
pleasure grounds around here

a long walk no syncopated
climax/crescendo cakewalk even if Sidney Bechet's leading the
    cakewalking band.

William Bartram in his travels in
the Cherokee country
often abandoned/alone in his situation

dejected/unharmonious all alone in wild Indian country
objects nonetheless conspired to conciliate
in some degree compose his
mind

"a new and
singularly beautiful" Aesculus pavia the singular red buckeye tree

"a new and beautiful" magnolia producing a rosaceous perfectly
    white flower of
a most fragrant scent in the center of a radius
of very large leaves

a company of young/innocent
Cherokee virgins "a gay assembly of hamadryades" picking
    strawberries
who confidently discovered themselves half unveiling their
blooming faces

merrily telling him
their fruit was ripe and sound and with native innocence
and cheerfulness presented little baskets
of their ripe and sound fruit.

7 3

Hama = with drus
= tree

a hamadryad a nymph living with/within a tree.

7 4

A contrary picture a photograph to illustrate the picture

Marilyn Monroe in a wedding dress and heels embracing trying
    to embrace
a tree
too blonde too late

to be a nymph.

7 5

Another contrary picture a Phyllis picture to illustrate the picture

trunk stem bole
of a tree parted/split wide open right down
the middle

flowering almond killed to the
ground.

Sign at a mega-store in the south of France "nothing beats a
virgin"

nothing beats parthenogenesis
poco a poco as may be.

Re case no. 343 some deductions

surroundings answer questions two blue mountains house in a
   row of houses
a church a bordello

wasn't a St. Louis woman with her diamond ring

she had profound needs

needs are motives

a most profound although not the only motive white as clarity
   after
the facts this is the modern motive

a profound need to be addressed without a dress

her heart didn't belong to daddy she wasn't her mother's daughter she was a reader

a narrow space is a fact local colors are facts two blue mountains
    are two big facts

opportunity = reading classics illustrated

she read in her own way with propriety not for the point for the
    picture the
truer identity she wasn't sequacious

her own way a modern way

naked/nakedly

didn't wish to be a sophisticated little lady didn't wish to tamper
or to be tampered with

Presbyterians don't handle snakes in church

you can be reborn you can have a profound need to be reborn but
    it's preferable
to be reborn in your own way with propriety with some a little

not wearing a see-through dress to church

not humming your own tune too loudly or worse
going hysterical/to pieces in the upper and extreme upper register
    of the voice
in church

time the most profound of all the profound needs

means/the weapon = the mind/her mind what perceives
the truer A = B truth what
tears off the veil the mind/her mind what veils and tears off veils
    over a long time

tenderness too is a motive

sin is not a red-headed woman sin is something else is not looking
    when
a woman chooses to be looked at/addressed

choice is invisible
with repetition choice's visible/clear
if a remembered body audacious white body descends a staircase
    this time you'd better
look

means/the weapon = the mind/her mind + propriety + persistence
    to make
the truer magic progress the change over a long time

nobody loved her

she didn't undergo total immersion in public in the Susquehanna

she wasn't the hyacinth girl

"A Tisket a Tasket" is a little tune it wasn't her tune

a girl a young woman a woman on a long progress needs to avoid
    breakdowns

a long progress all the stages an entire life.

7 8

Ten little questions running round the junior detective's brain no
    case being completely
closed

does need make the right to use

is agony frugal

what's the use of memory

is sorrow what floats your boat

does the body have a part to play in all apprenticeships

can the environment be resisted

disintegration resisted

must vision be penetrating won't you see more than you want to
    see

didn't a blonde get Paul Gonsalves going through twenty-seven
    straight choruses

is no whiteness so white as whiteness lost.

7 9

+ six little questions

what's the meaning of patience and what's all the good it brings

who was Jane Colden

why did the Holland case put Maigret in such a bad mood

what about the dative and what about touched

is pleasure the measure

can it have that swing and still not mean anything.

8 0

And one to grow on the as the heart grows older the colder
    question
what's love what's love got what's love got to do with it.

Some deductions cont.

wasn't a frail wasn't a weak sister

she was an animal a tigress of persistence

in her own words "a mysterious constant perseverance"
in her own words "I just persist"

no. 343 a special case not a sad case/the exception

red/auburn-haired

she had two breasts a freckled bosom

the body her body

who done it she done it.

Naturally, the exceptions have a very unhappy childhood and
youth, for to be essentially reflective at an age which is naturally
immediate is the most profound melancholy. But it has its return.
Most people drift on so as never to become spirit; all the many

happy years of their immediacy tend towards spiritual sluggish-
ness and so they never become spirit. But the unhappy childhood
and youth of the exceptions are transfigured into spirit.

8 3

Into spirit a
spirit of the place what's around here a spirit
of romance a nymph.

8 4

Zhiliao

cicada sound and Chinese sound for understanding
a later deduction "near
siren" = but not finally/at last a siren.

8 5

Neither the eiresione nor the daphnephoria
bringing myself to the tree to
her
a nymph unveiled

bringing myself humming to myself what the Raylettes insist
on so intensely insist on

"tell the truth" they really tear into it/bear down on it

why don't you tell the truth why not
the truth.

8 6

Zhiliao

but no siren not one of Bessie's girls not one of Tullio
    Lombardo's girls the hookers
and the haunters.

8 7

William Bartram in his travels in
the Cherokee country

conciliated in some degree by an assembly of gay hamadryads

William Bartram
left it to the person "of feeling and sensibility"
to form an idea of what lengths his passions hurried him

"thus
warmed and excited"

hurried him/his steps = hamadryads = nymphs hurried him/his
    steps

Graham Stuart Thomas "single trees . . . should lead to
the spinneys and woods"

a single tree

a single/singular nymph with/within

leads
conducts me to the
woods to what's further/beyond as after the tree

the woods which = memory

without a nymph means emphatically alone so lonesome
you could cry and who hasn't cried and cried when without
    motivation when without
animation/reanimation

form an idea a picture of what leads me

nymph with/within the tree not
end or final aim

not the end of my story but an effort to tell the truth of what's
further/beyond far into the woods.

88

Zhiliao

but not a girl who collects bones for a hobby
who wants all of you all of your bones your body and soul bones
all to herself for her
collection.

89

Wilson somewhere in western China
a storm brewing and the light rapidly failing impossible
to take a photograph

"though no photograph . . . would give an adequate idea of the
    grandeur of
the . . . scene"

"such scenes sink deep into the memory"

Bartram and Wilson and the others
nature boys and admirable men admirable and attentive Wilson
    ever curious as to
whether the feet of women were bound or "natural"

70

admirable/attentive in their explorations

in their pursuit motivated
by white
however shadowed by rejection by failure and flight

often abandoned all alone in their situations

in their pursuit of identification of understanding of new
life/living forms

my own steps ridiculous in
comparison

what could be more ridiculous

than exploring one's own woods the prosaic the familiar
the more so when between the end of winter and spring when the
    bluebells
cover the ground still not here
the ground muddy littered with indifferent mid-season colors

what more dangerous than memory
the prosaic the familiar the wholly lacking in scenes of grandeur
    neither China nor the
Cherokee country the bluebells electric in their ephemeral
    blueness
still not here

the ground muddy littered with indifferent colors

than finding/refinding
first love's lost love's body in the curving/recurving contours of
    a meander

what has been long prepared for what
cannot be prepared for

the sudden the moment subitane moment

shallow pools of water dull
leaves caught in the water bare brambles/multiflora on
the banks

no photograph
no photograph would

this is far into the woods where the deer hide from the hunters

a meander a mirror

what
I see a body "al hoolly her figure" a whole body/figure held back
    and withdrawn
all held back and withdrawn

what
I see a face of sorrow a young man's intense face "of sorwe so grete
    woon"

the truth

this is far into the woods and this is
liberation.

ODOR OF QUINCE

1

As sound it's Lester it's Lester Young returned/never gone leaping
    in but
gently
gentle tongue on the reed

in rapport with the body of the note

warm and tender enough body as if that body were about to
    awaken
an arm unwound a leg unbent

as if curve of the arm as if curve of the leg were about to become
    one curve unwinding and
unbending a sigh
from an about to awaken recumbent body

there must be a French word for it
because the note's one note one and only long opening sigh note
    of a French tune

désinvolture

tongue on that word ribbon-candy contour of its vowels
given extension/extending without constraint

beats forgotten bar lines forgotten
even Agnes Martin's shy/gossamer graph paper pencil lines curve
of the note extended going and going and beyond all that

gently warmly tenderly without lack of purpose purposive
   purposively

not the swirl of a stern Pompeian matron's mantle or
Judith Jamison's slow fan skirt or even the peacock
   display/flourishment of Johnny Hodges
this is Lester Young in rapport and ardemment

and this is one note long opening sigh
note then three notes

a triplet broken up each note stepped/spaced out a body's three
   exhalations

they fall away from the sigh of the one note

leaves from a tree in
late October/November

or one leaf which is the number 3 combined with that same
   number
but backwards
one leaf seen three ways

seen from one side from the other the other number 3

seen together/horizontally flagrant
lips

cascade/descent/glide of the notes like a song
Lester singing with Lady Day singing "Fine and Mellow" singing
    belle
et moelleuse

three notes which fall away in
their own curve
these three exhalations giving articulation to the given extension

then harp-tone/vibraphone glissandos
up and down the horn
in layers and layers chains of frills in the sashay of goldfish tails
    a loose/déshabillé
fabric
on which is scattered a scattered florilège of
    inflorescences/flowers without names and
simple stars
in a repeat/no repeat Moroccan rhythm getting quiet
getting quieter microtonal flowers and stars between repeat/
no repeat rests until the air itself breathes with a repeat/no repeat
    breath.

2

As color considered as a car a pink Cadillac

customized
the whole thing taken apart/stripped down to the essential
    torse/torso

where the car came from the luxe calme and volupté junkyard
where the job gets done where else it can only be
Rothko's body shop

a long job it takes a careful Rothko kind of character you have to
    know what you're doing
careful and serious
twenty-three coats of pink is serious

one after or on another one coat which is lightly sanded/hand-
    rubbed another
coat lightly sanded/hand-rubbed
twenty-three coats

a long job it takes time for a coat to dry
you have to take a break take your time step back sit down have
    a smoke

you have to think about it

if
it's to be not "like new" but new
but a new vehicle of transport and delight

and not Renoir's rosy-cheeked bather or Matisse's
rosy all over/flamingo chaise longue chaise lounge easy chair
or de Kooning's woman with a hat with a wet-on-wet cherry
    jubilee cake frosting skirt

if it's to be
a new vehicle no chrome

pink after or on participial pink

each coat thin as a film a film that's been diluted
with solvent
pigment particles almost disassociated from the film barely
    clinging
to the surface that's been sanded/hand-rubbed when light hits
    the particles
it bounces back suffusing the surface which is twenty-three
    surfaces which are becoming no surface/light
becoming the emergent impingement of pink light itself

a long job and
risky it's risky to ignore the limits of
physical coherence a Cadillac car the female form the chemistry of
    paint

it's risky to take apart/strip down

to ignore to take leave of/walk away from
all that's been loved and to leave pink light all by itself

which needs some blue
some blue underlining as a bar for a dancer to help make stable what

cannot be stable/is motile to help give some arabesque/Arabian
    motility to the motility

which needs a fresco a whole wall of purple which
comes from an oasis an orchard dream trunks and tree branches
along a path a stream
the trees are porches/portals a parade approaching a parenthetical
    moon
there's a body
undecorative body of a woman empurpled on
a nonornamental ground
that is the ripeness of all that is ripeness slumbering purple body
    key to the dream and to the
whole adamant mood of a fresco a wall

which makes the impingement more than an impingement
giving it drama ballets and divertissements depths and subtleties
    sensual
summonings.

3

As sign apprehended a new sign carved
by a tramp

a person who tramps/moves about "le voyageur fondamental"

fundamentally a gypsy surviving like a gypsy surviving
though no thief of
chickens or of children

like old Schimmel the woodcarver though
unbearded not an aesthetical beard communing with
    nature/wind in the windchime
pines to commune with a convex/so complex self

not a noble scholar beard on a leopard skin rug under an elegantly
    dripping
willow or an heroical beard
astride a craggy promontory heroically confronting ocean
    spray/the spraying surf in a suit

a tramp a person recognizable from childhood a childhood
    snapshot

blanket over his shoulder tied with binder-twine among taller
than him dusty hollyhocks

what a gypsy a tramp who has nothing has

an animal alertness to signs to changes in the weather what's
in the air

what a gypsy a tramp a carver
does carves

what's in the air makes room/space for what will be a new sign in
the air

one and only long opening sigh
body's
exhalations
harp-tone/vibraphone glissandos chains of frills inflorescences
flowers simple
stars in a repeat/no repeat Moroccan rhythm
pink needing some blue
not some little girl blue on a fresco a whole wall of purple an oasis
an orchard dream
slumbering empurpled body a dream a mood
a structure of mood
depths and subtleties summonings
emerging from that structure from a more than emergent pink
impingement

what a carver does

carves "from nature" a likeness thinks about it takes his
time many mornings perhaps years

carves again the work of a moment after many mornings/years

Mr. Johnson the pipemaker said his hands went so fast he didn't
    know what
they were doing

directement/straight
into sounds colors makes room/space for and makes a new sign the
shadow of

of what was given to him
in his voyaging/moving about of the shadow of a
smile

what a carver a gypsy a tramp does leaves

a given for what was given a new sign in the air immediate and
    intimate and though
no thief or shepherd either and must be/is moving on.

SHOW AND TELL/ROBERT CREELEY

Aspen the
'60s

where/when everything happened the beginning

when I first heard Coltrane
and saw something

Bobby Byrd said it was a good poem he was from Memphis and
    ought to know

when a gamin-faced girl came running from an airplane with her
    arms
outstretched

this is me then young man young poet
beside the Roaring Fork or a tributary the open blue and white
    For Love book in one hand
the other in a gesture of appeal

the assignment show and tell show what
you love

this poem "A Song"

fine clockwork of it subtle grammar of it of its words
their sounds and arrayment
Monk/Mozart refinement of the shifting pitches of this poem all
    fitted together quiet and
quiet

and unheard/cannot be heard over the white noise steady roar of
    the churned
up white water

hear me now all these years later

having spent the years in the song in the song/life business
having
paid dues

reading with older/different eyes
which see what they see through/after tears the locked the
    unacknowledged

unlocked
it is the learning of the meaning of the blues

help you see something see something you didn't see before

which is what is wanted in this poem which is a song and what
    the several requirements are

a grace
a song requires a girl so bright/in bloom who rejoices the heart

to whom one
gives gifts gives a diversity of gifts

a sign
the life of which is its use

which is Wittgenstein *The Blue & Brown Books* which was our
    conversation then Toby
and I when I arrived/right off
the bus young men on unpaved/dirt streets of the silver town

the life of which
is its use as adornment a gift among a diversity of gifts

a poet's thinking the long labor with words
the tenses
want wanted have/had wanted not what a young man was so
    wanting and wanting but what a
song wants just a few a spoonful of the right the rough and the
    smooth
words in the right order here and
there a rest making room for breath and letting a few of the words
    sink in

careful/with care how a song is to be sung if one sings it and
the last of the requirements

for *care is clear* having come through the ambiguities/tears having
    had to learn the meaning
of the blues

what will fit on a bracelet a simple inscription

all these years later
.hear me now having stepped back and needing to come forward

this poem is a song an
act
a work of love.

CADENZA 2

There are birds there is birdsong
unmourning and unmournful in the white light

there are birds there is birdsong
having come through hunger and danger
there is
free song a free weaving of many songs

song against song and other songs in a blending of wavy pitches

there are birds there is birdsong
unmourning and unmournful having come through

like the light like
like love never for sale.

CADENZA 3

There are birds

there are birds

there are birds

A NOTE & ACKNOWLEDGMENTS

To readers of these poems: it helps if they are read aloud.
You will occasionally come upon internal space gaps of varying
proportions (varying durations of silence). Please do not ignore
them. They provide time for rest, for an image to assume
depth and definition, for reflection. They are not so much
"holes" as cadenced parts of the whole that is each poem.

"Unveiling/Marianne Moore" includes quotations
from the following sources: section 19, Anne Carson,
Eros the Bittersweet (Dalkey Archive, 1998); sections 51, 52,
53, and 54, Simone Weil, *Waiting for God*, translated by
Emma Craufurd (Perennial Classics, 2001); section 82,
Søren Kierkegaard, *Papers and Journals: A Selection*,
translated by Alastair Hannay (Penguin, 1996).

Poems in this collection first appeared in the
following journals: *Cincinnati Review, Conjunctions,
Golden Handcuffs Review,* and *Origin* (online). Sections
from an earlier version of "Unveiling/Marianne Moore"
were first published by Atticus/Finch as a chapbook.

John Taggart is the author of a dozen previous volumes
of poetry, including *Crosses: Poems 1992–1998* (Stop Press, 2006)
and *Pastorelles* (Flood Editions, 2004). He has also published
two books of criticism, *Remaining in Light: Ant Meditations
on a Painting by Edward Hopper* (SUNY Press, 1993) and
Songs of Degrees: Essays on Contemporary Poetry and Poetics
(The University of Alabama Press, 1994). He lives in the
Cumberland Valley of south-central Pennsylvania.